AF228524

LA GALAXY

BY ANTHONY K. HEWSON

SportsZone

An Imprint of Abdo Publishing
abdobooks.com

abdobooks.com

Published by Abdo Publishing, a division of ABDO, PO Box 398166, Minneapolis, Minnesota 55439. Copyright © 2022 by Abdo Consulting Group, Inc. International copyrights reserved in all countries. No part of this book may be reproduced in any form without written permission from the publisher. SportsZone™ is a trademark and logo of Abdo Publishing.

Printed in the United States of America, North Mankato, Minnesota
052021
092021

Cover Photo: Danny Moloshok/AP Images
Interior Photos: Kevork Djansezian/AP Images, 5; Chris Carlson/AP Images, 6; Jae C. Hong/AP Images, 8, 20; Frederic J. Brown/AFP/Getty Images, 10–11; Bret Hartman/AP Images, 13; George Brich/AP Images, 15; Chris Martinez/AP Images, 16; Gary Friedman/Los Angeles Times/Getty Images, 19; Ric Tapia/AP Images, 23; Chris Pizzello/AP Images, 25; Mark J. Terrill/AP Images, 26; Kyle Rivas/Cal Sport Media/AP Images, 29; Aaron Lavinsky/Star Tribune/AP Images, 30; Scott Winters/Icon Sportswire/AP Images, 33; Stephen Dunn/Getty Images Sport/Getty Images, 35; Scott Halleran/Allsport/Getty Images Sport/Getty Images, 36; Doug Pensinger/Getty Images Sport/Getty Images, 39; Paul Chiasson/The Canadian Press/AP Images, 40; Tony Quinn/Icon Sportswire/AP Images, 42

Editor: Patrick Donnelly
Series Designer: Dan Peluso

Library of Congress Control Number: 2019954418

Publisher's Cataloging-in-Publication Data

Names: Hewson, Anthony K., author.
Title: LA Galaxy / by Anthony K. Hewson
Description: Minneapolis, Minnesota : Abdo Publishing, 2022 | Series: Inside MLS | Includes online resources and index.
Identifiers: ISBN 9781532192586 (lib. bdg.) | ISBN 9781644945667 (pbk.) | ISBN 9781098210489 (ebook)
Subjects: LCSH: Los Angeles Galaxy (Soccer team)--Juvenile literature. | Soccer teams--Juvenile literature. | Professional sports franchises--Juvenile literature. | Sports Teams--Juvenile literature.
Classification: DDC 796.334--dc23

TABLE OF CONTENTS

CHAPTER 1

BECKHAM BAGS A TITLE

Ask any American to name a soccer player during the early 2000s, and David Beckham was a likely choice. The English midfielder was a global superstar. And he put Major League Soccer (MLS) on the map when he joined the LA Galaxy in 2007. The team's ticket sales surged. Suddenly people around the world started to pay attention to soccer in the United States.

But Beckham didn't make the Galaxy winners. At least not early on. He was still an elite player. Even in his mid-30s, Beckham's amazing passing ability frustrated defenses and created scoring chances for the Galaxy. But going into the 2011 season, he was nearing the end of his career and had yet to lead the Galaxy to a title.

The Galaxy held a ceremony to welcome David Beckham to Los Angeles in 2007.

Landon Donovan, *left*, and Beckham formed a deadly one-two punch for the Galaxy.

Some fans had also gotten frustrated with Beckham. Upon joining the Galaxy, he was still aiming to make England's team for the 2010 World Cup. To improve his chances, Beckham chose to play on short-term loan deals with Italian club AC Milan before the 2009 and 2010 MLS seasons. However, those stretches caused him to miss the beginning of the MLS season. And in 2010, Beckham was injured while on loan and missed much of the Galaxy's season. Some fans questioned Beckham's commitment to the Galaxy and MLS.

COMING CLOSE

After missing the playoffs in Beckham's first two seasons, the Galaxy posted the best record in the Western Conference in 2009, 2010, and 2011. In 2009 they came achingly close to the MLS Cup title. Facing Real Salt Lake in the final, the match went to a penalty shootout. The Galaxy were defeated in the shootout 5–4.

GOING ALL IN

Things changed in 2011. The Galaxy were the league's most famous team. They had posted the league's best record in 2010. In Beckham and forward Landon Donovan, they had two of the league's best players. Now, with Beckham around all season, they were ready to take the next step.

Mike Magee celebrates his goal in the second leg of the MLS playoff series against New York in 2011.

The team started off well but struggled to string wins together. After a 2–1 loss to FC Dallas on May 1, LA found its form. The Galaxy went undefeated over their next 14 matches. One highlight was an incredible goal Beckham scored on July 9. He used his ball-bending ability to score directly off a corner kick, an extremely rare feat. The streak was snapped on August 3, but then the Galaxy didn't lose again until October.

The Galaxy received another boost that August with the arrival of Robbie Keane. The high-priced Irish forward had been a star in the English Premier League. He added even more firepower to the LA scoring attack.

But LA's playoff hero wasn't any of those big names. Mike Magee had been with the Galaxy since 2009. The forward had scored just five goals in the regular season. But the playoffs were a different story.

First, the Galaxy and the New York Red Bulls met in a two-legged series in the conference semifinals. In the opening leg at New York, Magee scored the lone goal of the match. Then back in Los Angeles for the second match, Magee scored again, and Donovan clinched it on a penalty kick as LA advanced. Magee then scored the game winner in the conference finals over Real Salt Lake. His three goals in three

Donovan watches his shot elude the Houston goalkeeper for the only goal of the 2011 MLS Cup.

playoff games earned Magee the nickname "Mr. November." The Galaxy would not have reached the MLS Cup without him.

CLAIMING THE CUP

In the MLS Cup, LA hosted the Houston Dynamo. An overflow crowd of more than 30,000 fans packed the Home Depot Center in Carson, California, to cheer on the Galaxy.

The match was tense. Neither team could find a way to score. But when the Galaxy finally broke through, all three of their megastars played key roles.

In the 72nd minute, Beckham went to the air. He used his head to flick the ball forward for Keane, who took off running. Keane weaved around a Houston defender. Then he passed the ball forward, right into Donovan's path.

Donovan ran in alone on the goalkeeper. He lightly tapped the ball, perfectly placing it just out of the keeper's reach. A Houston defender chased after the ball. But he was too late. The home crowd roared in celebration of the 1–0 lead.

The Galaxy almost scored again minutes later. Houston had one chance to tie it, but otherwise did not threaten the goal. LA ran out the clock to clinch its third MLS Cup victory.

Beckham turned to face the fans and celebrate with them. Donovan dropped to his knees. They then went to celebrate with the rest of the team. Beckham's contract was officially up after the season. But the fans begged their superstar to return.

"We want Beckham!" was the chant from behind the goal. Beckham wasn't ready to decide on his future just yet. But he had already given the fans memories for a lifetime.

A triumphant Beckham happily hoists the MLS Cup after the Galaxy's 2011 championship victory.

CHAPTER 2

A GALAXY IN THE CITY OF STARS

Soccer in Los Angeles dates back to the early 1900s. That was when the Greater Los Angeles Soccer League (GLASL) was founded. None of the teams were professional. But the matches were highly competitive no matter the stakes.

Los Angeles has long been a city of immigrants, and many of the GLASL teams were formed by immigrant groups. Teams such as the Los Angeles Scots and LA Armenians represented their communities.

One of the most successful teams was Maccabi Los Angeles. The team was formed in the 1970s by a group of Jewish Holocaust survivors. The Maccabees became just the second team to win five US Open Cup titles.

Superstar George Best of Northern Ireland, right, stands next to British rock star Elton John, part owner of the Los Angeles Aztecs, before a 1976 match.

TV star Andrew Shue was an all-conference player at Dartmouth College before he joined the Galaxy.

That tournament, which has now held more than 100 editions, is open to any team in the United States.

Eventually pro soccer began to edge out regional leagues like the GLASL for attention. The Los Angeles Wolves won the United Soccer Association (USA) title in 1967. The next year, the USA merged with the National Professional Soccer League to form the North American Soccer League (NASL). The Wolves folded after one NASL season. But the Los Angeles Aztecs joined the league in 1974 and won the championship in their first season.

The Aztecs were the West Coast version of the New York Cosmos. The Cosmos brought in famous players such as Brazilian icon Pelé to add to the star power of the league. The Aztecs took a similar approach. They signed legendary European players George Best of Northern Ireland and Johan Cruyff of the Netherlands.

But US interest in soccer began to wane by the early 1980s. The Aztecs folded in 1981. The rest of the NASL went the same way in 1984. But pro soccer didn't go away for long. As part of a successful bid for the 1994 World Cup, the United States promised to establish a new top-tier professional soccer league. That's how Major League Soccer was born.

AN MLS ORIGINAL

The LA Galaxy were one of the original 10 teams when the league debuted in 1996. Like the other teams in the league, they wore bold-colored uniforms. LA's were an electric mix of green, yellow, and orange. And the Galaxy name has two meanings. Just like a Galaxy is home to stars, Los Angeles is home to its own "stars" in the form of celebrities.

The Galaxy had an actual Hollywood star on the 1996 team. Andrew Shue was an actor on the popular television show *Melrose Place*. And he was also a soccer player. To help promote the new league, he played in five games with the Galaxy, recording one assist. But the Galaxy had full-time soccer stars, too. Midfielders Mauricio Cienfuegos and Cobi Jones kept the machine running smoothly. The Galaxy made it all the way to the MLS Cup, though they lost to the league's first dominant team, DC United.

Cobi Jones, *right*, scores the Galaxy's second goal in their Concacaf Champions' Cup final victory over Olimpia.

In the early days, LA was frequently one of the top teams in the Western Conference, but it could not break through to win a championship. After losing another MLS Cup in 1999, the team won its first trophy, the Concacaf Champions' Cup, in January 2001. Now known as the Concacaf Champions League,

The stars were aligned when the Galaxy fielded a lineup featuring Robbie Keane, Landon Donovan, and David Beckham.

the competition features the best club teams from throughout North America, Central America, and the Caribbean. The Galaxy beat Olimpia of Honduras 3–2 in the final, with Ezra Hendrickson scoring the winning goal. Twenty years later, the Galaxy were still the last MLS team to win the tournament.

Meanwhile, the Galaxy showed off their national superiority by winning the US Open Cup for the first time in 2001. In 2002 the team finally broke through with an MLS trophy, winning the MLS Cup 1–0 over the New England Revolution.

The arrival of Landon Donovan sparked a resurgence for LA. Donovan was a superstar for the US men's national team. The Galaxy won both the US Open Cup and the MLS Cup in 2005.

THE BECKHAM ERA

The Galaxy already had many standouts in their short history. But MLS teams couldn't afford the best players in the world, most of whom played in Europe. That changed in 2007. The team took a big risk in signing English midfielder David Beckham. Beckham was one of the most famous athletes in the world. The league had to change its rules to allow the Galaxy to go over the salary cap to sign Beckham. This became known as the "Beckham Rule," and it has expanded over time.

Beckham's early years were rocky on the field. But his presence brought a lot of attention and interest to the Galaxy and MLS as a whole. And by 2009, the Galaxy had become contenders. Donovan, Beckham, and new addition Robbie Keane formed a fearsome trio that dominated the league in 2011. LA won back-to-back MLS Cups in 2011 and 2012.

Beckham left the Galaxy after the 2012 season. Donovan and Keane led the team to another MLS Cup in 2014, and then Donovan temporarily retired. Many more changes followed in the years to come.

Donovan had come out of retirement briefly to help the team make the playoffs in 2016. But the end of the 2016 season saw the departure of head coach and general manager Bruce Arena, who left to coach the US men's national team. Also gone were Keane, longtime defender Omar Gonzalez, and Donovan again.

All the changes were too much, and the Galaxy finished last in MLS in 2017. The team responded in 2018 by adding Swedish superstar Zlatan Ibrahimović. The confident striker stayed just two years but helped the Galaxy reach the playoffs in 2019. A new superstar, Javier "Chicharito" Hernández, arrived in 2020. The moves showed stars still wanted to play with the Galaxy, but leading the team back to the top proved more challenging.

High-scoring striker Zlatan Ibrahimović joined the Galaxy in 2018.

CHAPTER 3

HEROES OF
THE GALAXY

It was hard to miss Cobi Jones. With his dreadlocks and enthusiastic personality, Jones was a star on the US national team. He scored the first goal in Galaxy team history. He went on to score 82 for the team before retiring in 2007. He was also a part of two MLS Cup championship teams.

Jones was a midfielder but had the versatility to play like a forward. More than a decade after he retired, Jones remained third in team history in goals and first all time in games played (392) and assists (111). After retiring, Jones served as a Galaxy assistant coach for three years. He later moved into the announcers' booth, providing analysis on Galaxy TV broadcasts. Jones was inducted into the team's Ring of Honor for his service to the club.

Cobi Jones (13) was one of the most famous US soccer players in the 1990s and 2000s.

Mauricio Cienfuegos, *left*, was one of the Galaxy's early stars.

Mauricio Cienfuegos was another original Galaxy player who ended up in the team's Ring of Honor. The Salvadoran midfielder stood just 5-foot-6 and weighed 140 pounds. But he played like a giant. Cienfuegos was the team's main playmaker. His crisp and creative passes helped unlock defenses and led to many Galaxy goals. He made 206 appearances for LA from 1996 to 2003.

Kevin Hartman was a steady presence between the posts from 1997 to 2006. Because of his agility and acrobatic saves, he was nicknamed *El Gato*, Spanish for "the cat." Hartman made 243 appearances for the Galaxy and was named MLS Goalkeeper of the Year in 1999.

A HOMETOWN STAR

Landon Donovan was already an international soccer star when he signed with his hometown Galaxy in 2005. In 2002 he and the US men's national team made it all the way to the quarterfinals of the World Cup.

NATIONAL TEAM BOSSES

The Galaxy have had many famous players. They also have had some of the top managers in American soccer. Two Galaxy head coaches have also coached the US men's national team. Steve Sampson coached the Galaxy to the 2005 MLS Cup title. He also led the men's national team at the 1998 World Cup. Bruce Arena was the greatest coach in Galaxy history, winning MLS Cup titles in 2011, 2012, and 2014. He also coached the national team to the 2002 World Cup quarterfinals and has the most wins in program history.

Donovan was named the tournament's best young player. But he had yet to find a comfortable home at the club level.

After struggling with a German team, Donovan found the Galaxy to be the perfect fit. Donovan, who grew up in nearby Ontario, California, led the club in goals six times. He was the MLS Most Valuable Player (MVP) in 2009, an award that now bears his name. A talented playmaker at forward, Donovan was a natural scorer. His 141 goals for LA are by far the most in club history.

Donovan likely could have left LA to play overseas. But he chose to stay close to home. The only exceptions were short spells on loan to English club Everton, where he became a fan favorite. Donovan ended his career as one of the greatest American soccer players ever. He retired from the national team with 57 goals, tied for the most in team history.

GOING GLOBAL

Some players have as big of an impact off the field as they do on it. David Beckham was one of those players. On the field, Beckham made three All-Star teams, scored 18 goals, and led the Galaxy to two titles in his six MLS seasons.

Many observers consider Landon Donovan the best US-born soccer player in history.

Jonathan dos Santos starred for Mexico's national team and the Galaxy.

But off the field, his signing in 2007 was a historic moment for MLS. It showed the league could attract big stars. And fans responded. Attendance rose, TV ratings increased, and the league expanded by six teams from 2007 to 2012.

Although Beckham was the Galaxy's highest profile international signing, Robbie Keane might have been its most successful. "Keano" was fresh off a long stint in England where he was known as a dangerous scoring threat. He was the same in Los Angeles, leading the club in goals each year from 2012 to 2015. Keane also scored nine career playoff goals and was named the MVP of the Galaxy's victory over New England in the 2014 MLS Cup.

Team chemistry is vital to having success in soccer. Players must know the strengths and weaknesses of their teammates. Two Galaxy teammates in 2017 and 2018 had no problem in that area. They were brothers. Jonathan and Giovani dos Santos played together for two seasons in LA. They also played together on Mexico's national team. Though he led the team in goals in 2016, Giovani failed to live up to expectations and was released in 2019. Jonathan remained on the team and was a regular in midfield.

ANOTHER SHINING STAR

The latest star with the Galaxy joined the club in January 2020. Javier "Chicharito" Hernández is the all-time leading goal scorer for Mexico's national team. Chicharito had spent the previous 10 seasons playing in Europe's top-flight leagues. The Galaxy thought he'd be a perfect fit on and off the field. When he signed his contract, Chicharito said he was excited to play in a city with so many Mexican-American soccer fans.

By 2018 the Galaxy were in need of a jolt. They got just that when they convinced Zlatan Ibrahimović to leave Europe and bring his skills to the United States. The Swede was known for scoring big goals and carrying a big attitude. For example, upon signing with the Galaxy, Ibrahimović took out an ad in the local newspaper that simply read, "Dear Los Angeles, you're welcome."

As one of the greatest goal scorers ever, Ibrahimović could back up that display of confidence. He had scored more than 500 goals for club and country across a legendary career. With the Galaxy, though in his late 30s, Ibrahimović set a new club record with 30 goals in the 2019 season. Though he returned to Europe after just two memorable seasons, Ibrahimović once again showed that the game's biggest stars could thrive in Los Angeles.

"I came, I saw, I conquered," he wrote in a farewell Facebook post. "Thank you LA Galaxy for making me feel alive again."

Zlatan Ibrahimović was often the center of attention during his two seasons with the Galaxy.

CHAPTER 4

GREATEST GALAXY MOMENTS

MLS looked a lot different back in 1996. The Galaxy played their first game in multicolored uniforms in an American football stadium against a team whose name doesn't exist anymore. However, one element remains the same today— the enthusiasm of the hometown fans. Nearly 70,000 of them were on hand at the Rose Bowl on April 13, 1996.

LA played the New York/New Jersey MetroStars. Club legend Cobi Jones scored the first goal in team history. Later in the match, Galaxy keeper Jorge Campos threw a perfect ball to defender Arash Noamouz breaking out of his own zone. Noamouz worked his way through the MetroStars defense and fired a shot past the goalkeeper. The Galaxy held on for a 2–1 inaugural victory.

Galaxy defender Chris Armas, left, fights for the ball with the MetroStars' Edmundo Rodriguez on April 13, 1996.

Danny Califf was the hero when the Galaxy won the US Open Cup final in 2001.

The Galaxy did a lot of winning in 1996. LA made it all the way to the MLS Cup final against DC United. The match was played in driving rain and the field was soaked. But more than 37,000 fans still came out to Foxborough, Massachusetts, to watch. Everything looked sunny for the Galaxy as they raced out to a 2–0 lead. But three late United goals doomed LA, and DC won 3–2.

LA was still seeking its first MLS Cup. But in January 2001, it brought home a rare trophy. The Galaxy won the Concacaf Champions' Cup tournament that was played in Los Angeles. As the continental champs, the Galaxy qualified for the 2001 FIFA Club World Cup. A match against world power Real Madrid was set to be played in Spain. But the tournament was cancelled for financial reasons.

BECOMING CHAMPIONS

The Galaxy played a number of big matches in the 2000s. The New England Revolution were their opponents in many of them. The Galaxy and Revolution first met in a final in 2001. They were playing for the US Open Cup. Danny Califf scored an extra-time winner as the Galaxy lifted the trophy for the first time.

The Galaxy and Revolution met again in 2002. This time they were playing for the MLS Cup. Both team's defenses were strong, and it went into extra time 0–0. That's when Carlos Ruiz, who had been the Galaxy's top scorer all year, came through again. In the 113th minute, Ruiz received a crossing pass in the box. He calmly redirected it into the net, and the Galaxy were finally MLS champions.

The Galaxy were back in the MLS Cup final in 2005. And once again, their opponent was the Revolution. The game was a near repeat of the scoreless duel back in 2002. The scoreboard read 0–0 as the game headed into extra time. This time the Galaxy hero was midfielder Guillermo Ramírez. He had been loaned to the Galaxy during the season, but he hadn't had much of an impact on the offense. In fact, he had missed the target on 61 of the 62 shots he had taken that year. But his goal in the 107th minute gave the Galaxy a second MLS Cup.

Carlos Ruiz watches as his shot slips past the New England keeper and into the net to win the 2002 MLS Cup.

David Beckham brought international recognition and excitement to MLS when he joined the Galaxy in 2007.

The excitement that those two MLS Cup titles generated in Los Angeles was big, but it would be dwarfed by what was to come.

BECKHAM BUZZ

The frenzy in Los Angeles grew as July 21, 2007, drew closer. David Beckham was coming to Los Angeles. Beckham made his Galaxy debut at home in a friendly against England's Chelsea. All eyes in a record crowd were on Beckham, even though he was on the bench for most of the match. A TV camera was even assigned to stay on Beckham throughout the game.

It took a few years for the Galaxy to build a title contender with Beckham. But once they did, they dominated MLS. After losing the 2009 MLS Cup to Real Salt Lake, the Galaxy finally broke through in 2011. Beckham decided to play one more year in LA after that, and the Galaxy ended up back in the MLS Cup final. Their two other stars,

Robbie Keane scores the game-winning goal in the 2014 MLS Cup.

Landon Donovan and Robbie Keane, each scored on penalty kicks as the Galaxy won 3–1. It turned out to be Beckham's last game in MLS.

LA needed to find out if it could win without Beckham in 2014. Donovan and Keane proved they were more than enough. LA met old rivals New England for the MLS Cup. With the score 1–1 in extra time, Keane was the hero. He ran in alone in the 111th minute and laced a shot past the keeper. He then did his trademark cartwheel celebration in front of the home fans as the Galaxy became the first team to win five MLS Cups.

LA got a new rival when Los Angeles Football Club (LAFC) joined MLS in 2018. The Galaxy's new star, Zlatan Ibrahimović, welcomed LAFC with a legendary goal on March 31, 2018. It was also Ibrahimović's first Galaxy goal. It ended up being the MLS goal of the year. The ball fell to Ibrahimović a long distance from the goal, but he hammered a bending strike that rocketed past the keeper.

Over the years, the LA Galaxy has truly lived up to its name. The team has had some of the greatest stars in American soccer. They have given fans a universe full of memorable moments and trophies.

TIMELINE

1996	2001	2001	2002	2005
The Galaxy play their first game, a 2–1 home win over the New York/New Jersey MetroStars on April 13.	LA wins its first trophy, beating Olimpia of Honduras to take home the Concacaf Champions' Cup on January 21.	On October 27, the Galaxy win their first US Open Cup title with a 2–1 win over the New England Revolution.	LA breaks through to win its first MLS Cup title on October 20 with Carlos Ruiz scoring the lone goal in extra time to beat the Revolution 1–0.	LA captures a "double" by winning both the US Open Cup and the MLS Cup in the same season.

2007	2011	2012	2014	2019
The Galaxy sign English superstar David Beckham, whose MLS career spurs interest in the league and increased attendance throughout North America.	Beckham and the Galaxy win their first MLS Cup title together with a 1–0 victory over the Houston Dynamo on November 20.	The Galaxy repeat as MLS Cup champions, after which Beckham leaves MLS.	Robbie Keane scores in extra time to give the Galaxy a 2–1 MLS Cup win over New England on December 10. LA becomes the first team to win five MLS Cup titles.	In his second of two seasons in Los Angeles, legendary striker Zlatan Ibrahimović scores a team-record 30 goals and leads the Galaxy to the playoffs.

TEAM FACTS

FIRST SEASON

1996

STADIUMS

Rose Bowl, Pasadena, California (1996–2002)
Dignity Health Sports Park, Carson, California (2003–)

MLS CUP TITLES

2002, 2005, 2011, 2012, 2014

US OPEN CUP TITLES

2001, 2005

CONCACAF CHAMPIONS LEAGUE TITLES

2000

KEY PLAYERS

David Beckham (2007–12)
Landon Donovan (2005–14, 2016)
Omar Gonzalez (2009–15)
Kevin Hartman (1997–2006)
Zlatan Ibrahimović (2018–19)
Cobi Jones (1996–2007)
Robbie Keane (2011–16)

KEY COACHES

Bruce Arena (2008–16)
Steve Sampson (2004–06)
Sigi Schmid (1999–2004, 2017–18)

MLS MOST VALUABLE PLAYERS

Landon Donovan (2009)
Robbie Keane (2014)
Carlos Ruiz (2002)

MLS DEFENDER OF THE YEAR

Robin Fraser (1999)
Omar Gonzalez (2011)

MLS NEWCOMER OF THE YEAR

Zlatan Ibrahimović (2018)

MLS GOALKEEPER OF THE YEAR

Kevin Hartman (1999)
Donovan Ricketts (2010)

MLS HUMANITARIAN OF THE YEAR

A. J. DeLaGarza (2014)

MLS ROOKIE OF THE YEAR

Sean Franklin (2008)
Omar Gonzalez (2009)

MLS COMEBACK PLAYER OF THE YEAR

David Beckham (2011)

MLS COACH OF THE YEAR

Bruce Arena (2011)
Sigi Schmid (1999)

GLOSSARY

contender
A person or team that has a good chance at winning a championship.

corner kick
A free kick from a corner of the field near the opponent's goal.

ejected
Removed from a game, usually due to unsportsmanlike behavior.

extra time
Two 15-minute periods added to a game if the score is tied at the end of regulation.

forward
Also called a striker, the player who plays nearest the opponent's goal.

friendly
A match that is not part of league play or a tournament; an exhibition match.

loan
An agreement that allows a player to play for another team for a single season or less.

midfielder
A player who stays mostly in the middle third of the field and links the defenders with the forwards.

penalty kick
A play in which a shooter faces a goalkeeper alone; it is used to decide tie games or as a result of a foul.

salary cap
A limit on the amount of money that teams can pay players.

shootout
A tiebreaking procedure consisting of alternating penalty kicks to decide a game's winner.

MORE INFORMATION

BOOKS

Kortemeier, Todd. *Total Soccer*. Minneapolis, MN: Abdo Publishing, 2017.

Marthaler, Jon. *Ultimate Soccer Road Trip*. Minneapolis, MN: Abdo Publishing, 2019.

Trusdell, Brian. *Soccer Record Breakers*. Minneapolis, MN: Abdo Publishing, 2016.

ONLINE RESOURCES

To learn more about the LA Galaxy, please visit **abdobooklinks.com** or scan this QR code. These links are routinely monitored and updated to provide the most current information available.

INDEX

ABOUT THE AUTHOR

Anthony K. Hewson has followed soccer in Southern California since before the MLS days. Originally from San Diego, he now lives in the Bay Area with his wife and dogs.